I0816771

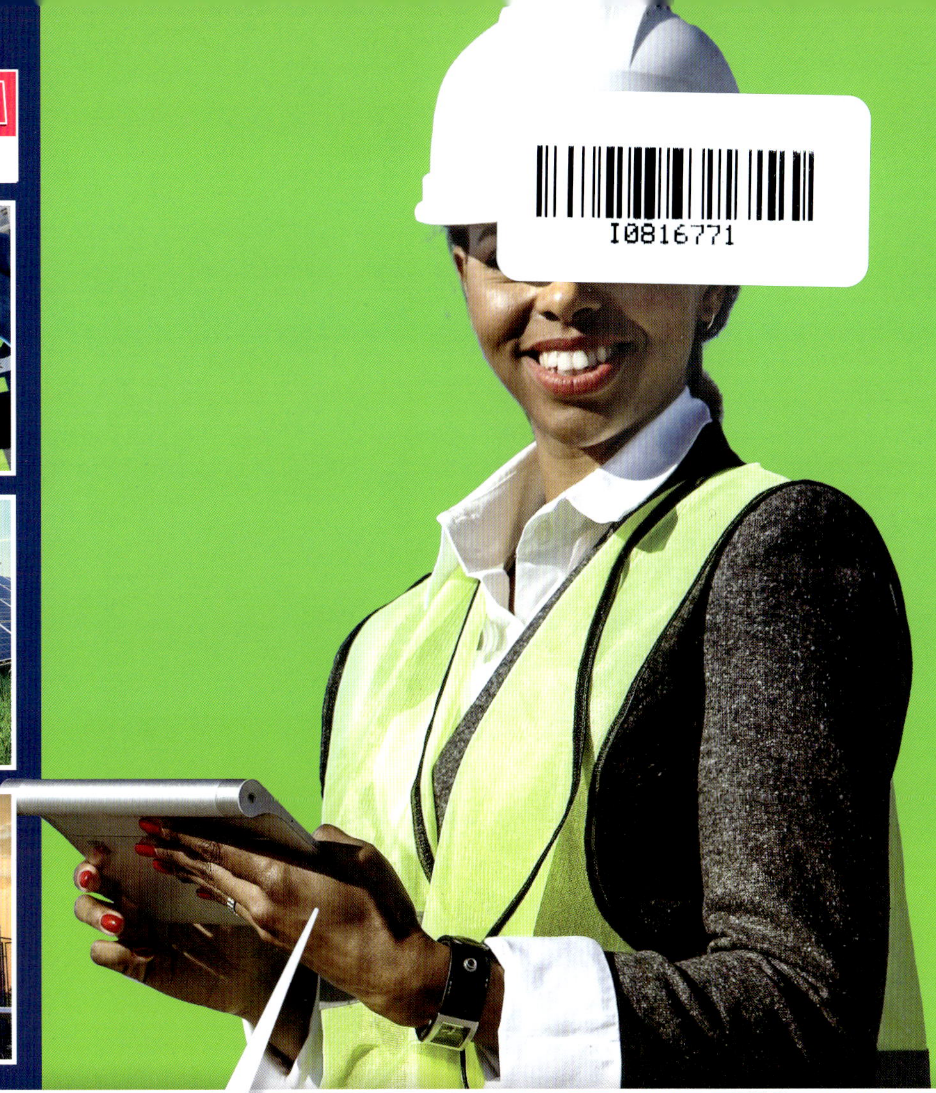

ENVIRONMENTAL ENGINEER

Tammy Gagne and
Heather Kissock

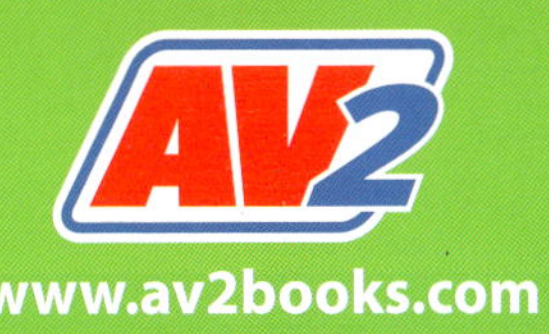

www.av2books.com

Step 1
Go to **www.av2books.com**

Step 2
Enter this unique code
FUBPYGRYI

Step 3
Explore your interactive eBook!

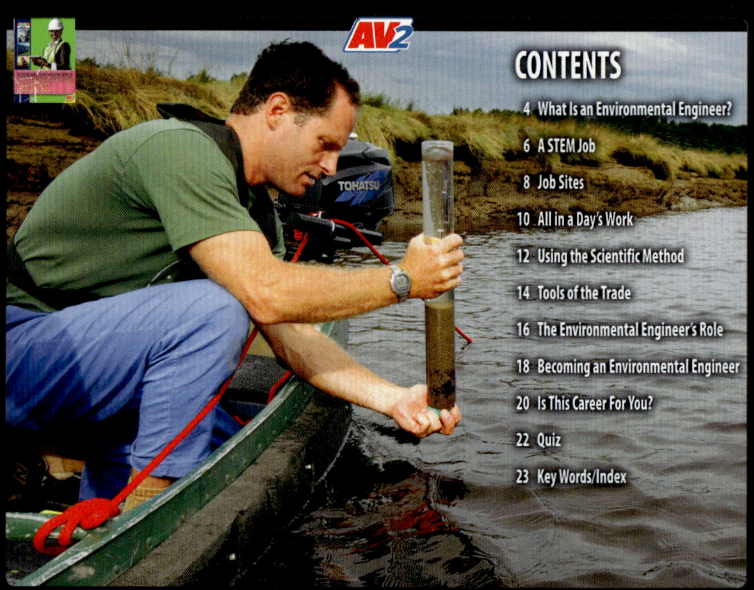

AV2 is optimized for use on any device

Your interactive eBook comes with...

Contents
Browse a live contents page to easily navigate through resources

Audio
Listen to sections of the book read aloud

Videos
Watch informative video clips

Weblinks
Gain additional information for research

Try This!
Complete activities and hands-on experiments

Key Words
Study vocabulary, and complete a matching word activity

Quizzes
Test your knowledge

Slideshows
View images and captions

... and much, much more!

View new titles and product videos at www.av2books.com

Careers

ENVIRONMENTAL ENGINEER

Contents

What Is an Environmental Engineer?

An environmental engineer is a person who develops ways to protect the environment. Every day, activities such as construction, manufacturing, and even driving release harmful chemicals into the air, water, and soil. The main goal of most environmental engineers is to reduce this pollution. Some of their work focuses on cleaning up pollution. They may also develop ways to prevent further **contamination** of Earth's **natural resources**.

Many environmental engineers work directly with large companies. They advise these companies on how to keep their **carbon footprint** as low as possible. Environmental engineers also work with governments to create laws that protect Earth's natural resources. Some environmental engineers perform inspections to make sure that companies follow these important standards.

More than **55,000** environmental engineers work in the **United States**.

The average **salary** of an environmental engineer in the United States is **$94,220**.

By 2024, the United States is expected to have about **62,000** environmental engineers, an **increase** of **12.4%** over the past 10 years.

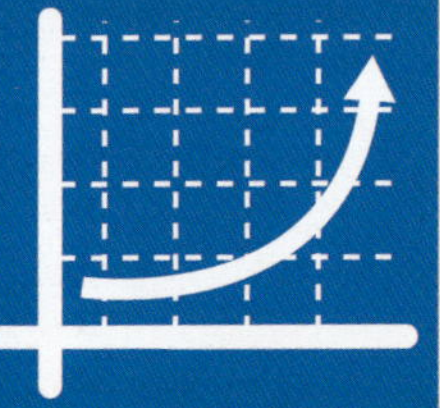

Environmental engineers are often required to test the toxicity levels of water, soil, and air. This requires specialized equipment and clothing.

A STEM Job

Environmental engineers work in the field of STEM. STEM stands for Science, Technology, Engineering, and Mathematics, or math. STEM is a developing field. Jobs in STEM change as new tools and techniques are created.

Most environmental engineers use all of the STEM subjects for their work. However, different types of environmental engineers may use one subject more than the others. Some environmental engineers create models of the environment to better understand **climate change**. These engineers rely on their math skills to create formulas and make calculations. A bio-environmental engineer uses more **biology**. This type of engineer works to reduce health risks in settings such as workplaces.

Where Environmental Engineers Work

Environmental engineers can be found in all 50 U.S. states. However, most jobs are concentrated in five states. The state with the highest number of environmental engineers is California.

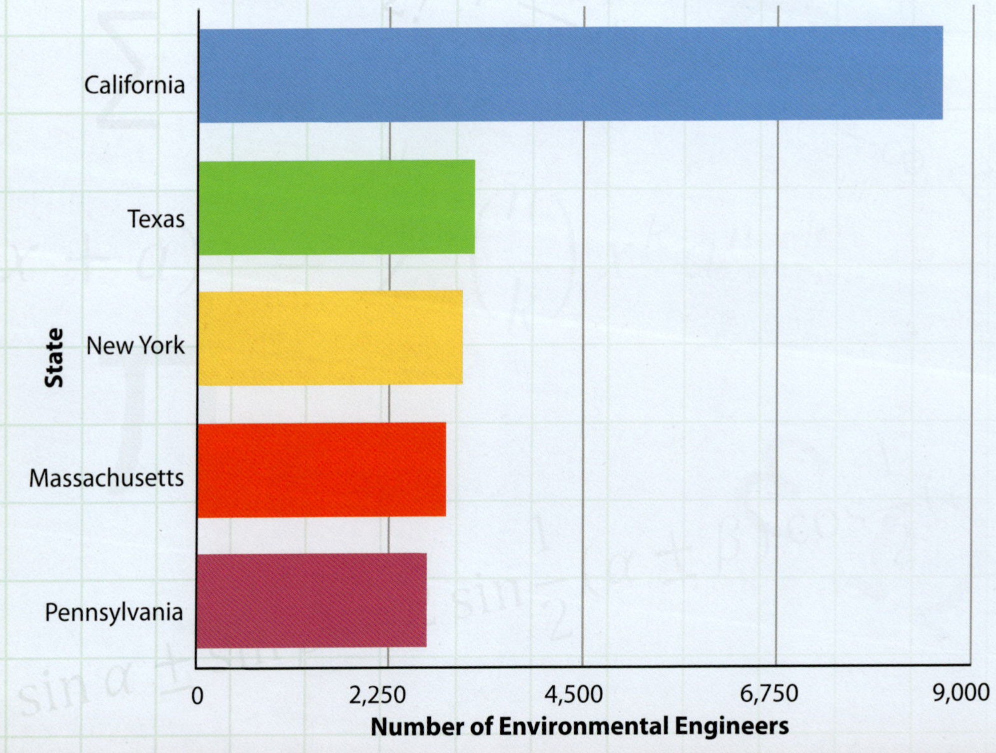

Many people in STEM jobs work with others in related fields. For instance, an environmental engineer who specializes in water resources might work with oceanographers or marine biologists. These people also work in STEM fields. Having a strong grasp of all STEM subjects can help make an environmental engineer more useful in a wider variety of specialties.

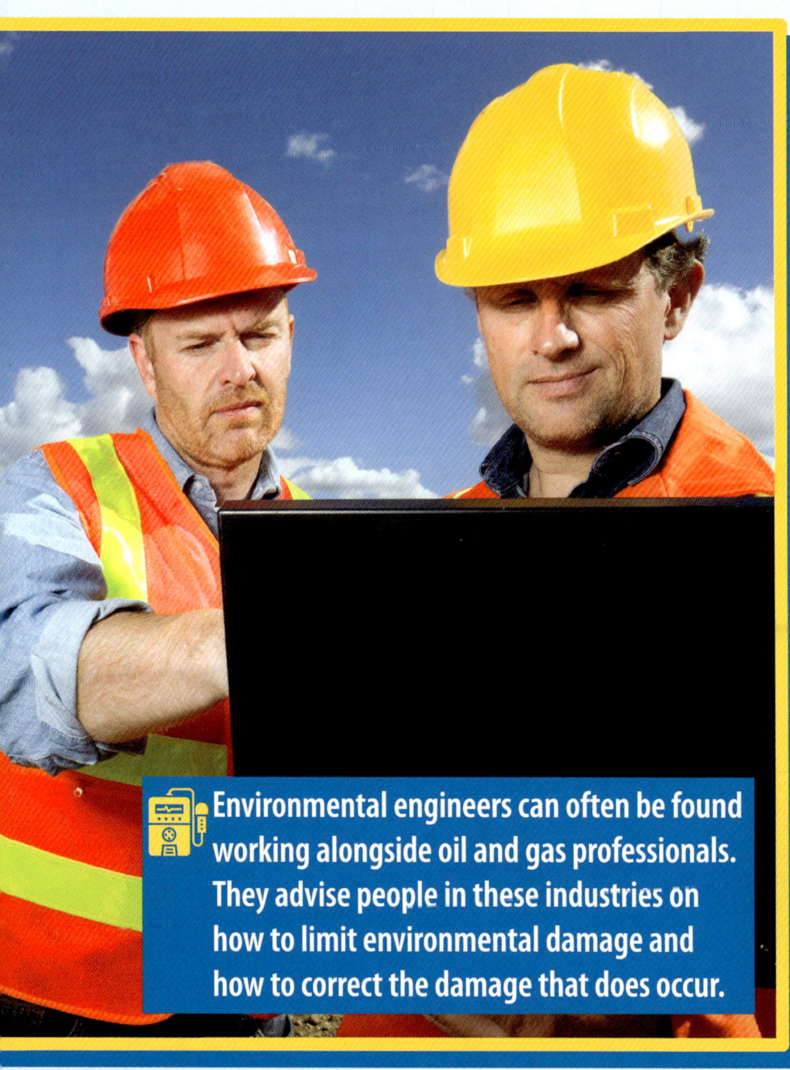

Environmental engineers can often be found working alongside oil and gas professionals. They advise people in these industries on how to limit environmental damage and how to correct the damage that does occur.

More than **70%** of environmental engineers are **male**.

The **average age** of an environmental engineer is **42.4**.

About 89% of environmental engineers are employed in **full-time jobs**.

Job Sites

Environmental engineers work for a wide range of companies and organizations. Most work for architecture firms or engineering firms. A large number work for state and local governments. Other environmental engineers may work for **laboratories**, industrial plants, or consulting companies.

Top Environmental Engineering Firms in the United States

Most major engineering firms in the United States have environmental engineers on staff. They provide valuable information on how to plan projects in ways that respect the environment.

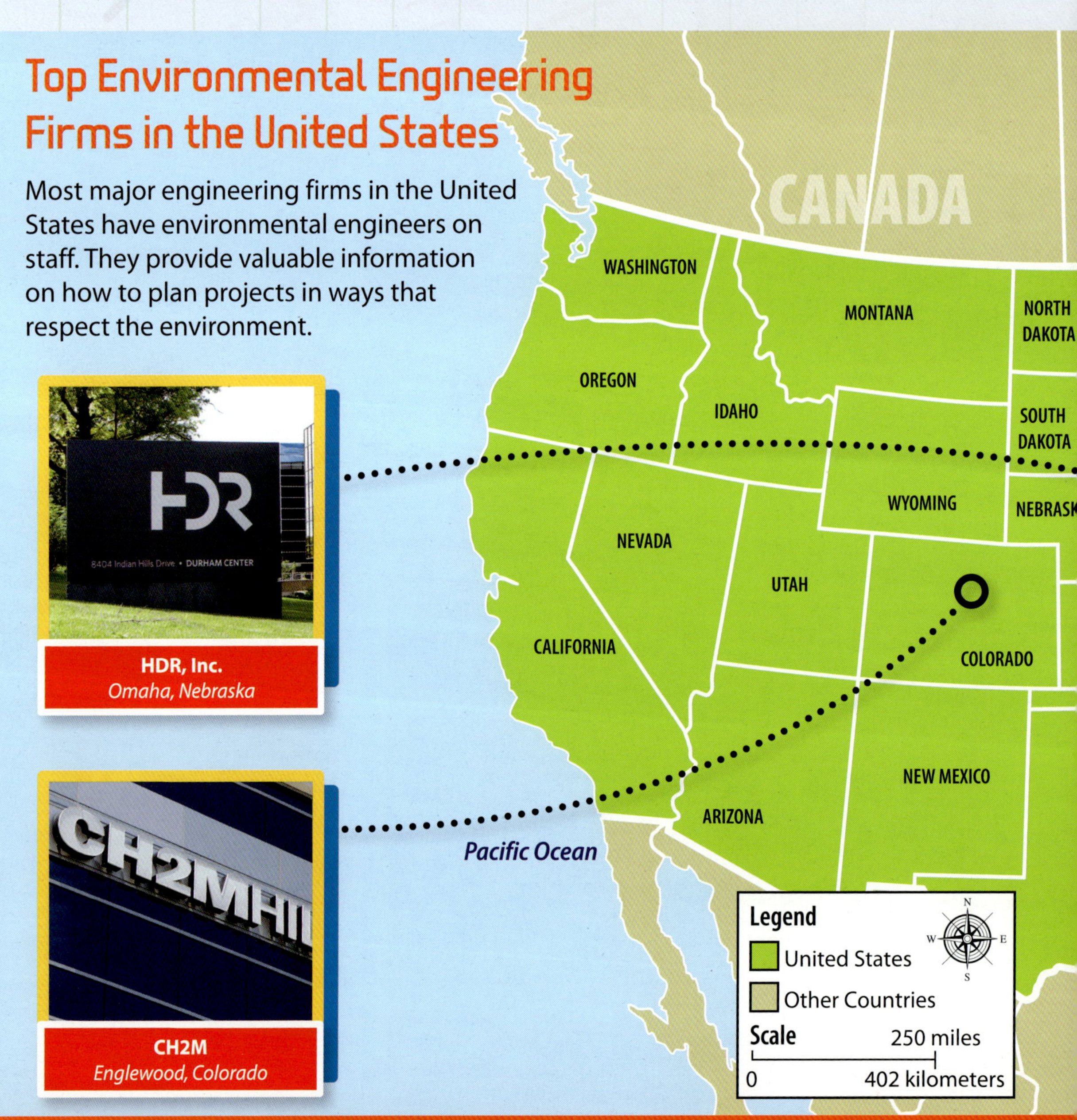

HDR, Inc.
Omaha, Nebraska

CH2M
Englewood, Colorado

Most environmental engineers are based in offices. However, their work often involves visiting other sites. Sometimes, this can take environmental engineers into risky surroundings. For instance, they may have to take samples from a **sewage** plant or test for **radiation** at a mine. Both tasks deal with dangerous substances. The environmental engineer must be aware of the risks involved and come to these sites prepared for what could happen.

CleanHarbors, Inc.
Norwell, Massachusetts

Jacobs Engineering Group
Dallas, Texas

Sample collection is one of an environmental engineer's main outdoor jobs. Sediment samples can be used to gauge the oxygen levels in waterways.

All in a Day's Work

Most environmental engineers divide their time between the office and the field. Some might schedule entire days indoors or outdoors. Others may prefer the variety of moving from one location to another in a single day.

The office is where environmental engineers perform the administrative and planning aspects of their job. On any given day, this can include working on design plans, arranging for permits, or reviewing building regulations. Outside the office, they may attend meetings or give presentations. Time in the field might be spent running tests, performing inspections, or supervising the installation of equipment.

Sample Daily Schedule

An environmental engineer must be ready to perform hands-on work in the field. He or she must also be skilled at reporting the **data** from this work to the people who need it.

8:00 AM

Upon arriving at the office, an environmental engineer begins to prepare for his role as an expert witness at an upcoming trial. A factory is believed to be releasing dangerous chemicals into the water supply. The engineer needs to review the data and plan the water testing he wants to conduct.

10:00 AM

The engineer meets with clients who want to open a restaurant on the site of an old gas station. The land is suspected of being a **brownfield**. The clients ask the engineer to take soil samples and report the results. They cannot get their permit to open the restaurant without this important step.

11:00 AM

The environmental engineer heads out to test the soil at a paper mill. His company acts as a consultant for the business. This means that it helps the mill comply with environmental regulations.

2:00 PM

After lunch, the engineer heads into his laboratory with the soil samples he gathered at the paper mill. He will be testing the soil for chemicals used in the papermaking process.

3:00 PM

The engineer meets with a client who wants to build on land that was once an orchard. The engineer agrees to test the soil to make sure it does not contain chemicals from the **pesticides** used to protect the orchard's crops. These chemicals could contaminate the water on the property.

4:00 PM

The engineer's final meeting for the day is with an architect. Together, they are designing a **wastewater treatment plant** for the city. The engineer's job is to make sure that the plant will meet current environmental regulations.

Using the Scientific Method

Scientists use the scientific method to solve problems. The scientific method is a series of steps. It begins with a question scientists want to answer. First, the scientists find out if someone else has asked the same question. If so, they review that scientist's results and gather information for their work. Next, they make a hypothesis. This is what they think the answer to their question will be. The scientists then test the hypothesis with an experiment. After the experiment, they form a conclusion. This means they study the results and decide if the question was answered. Finally, the scientists share the results with the public and other scientists.

1. Ask a Question

Is an oil spill difficult to clean up?

2. Construct a Hypothesis

Once chemicals enter water, they can be difficult to gather and remove. Cleaning them up as thoroughly as possible is a complex and time-consuming task.

3. Test with an Experiment

Begin by pouring 1 quart (0.95 liters) of water into a shallow baking dish. Mix 1 tablespoon of cocoa powder into 1 cup of vegetable oil. Slowly pour the oil mixture into the water. This will simulate the spill. Wait one minute for the oil to spread throughout the container. One at a time, use a paper towel, a cotton ball, and a spoon to try to remove the oil from the water.

4. Did the Test Work?

The test showed that each item was only able to remove a small amount of oil. There was still oil in the dish after all materials were used.

5. Draw Conclusions

The test indicates that an oil spill in a real waterway would be very difficult to clean up. This is why some environmental engineers' work focuses on finding ways to prevent oil spills from happening.

Tools of the Trade

Environmental engineers spend much of their time testing air, soil, and water for contaminants. When engineers find them, they need tools to remove these substances. This process is called remediation.

Water Quality Monitors

Environmental engineers use water quality monitors to see if a water supply contains dangerous chemicals. These handheld devices can sense and measure both safe and harmful substances in the water. They allow environmental engineers to solve water quality issues before they become much bigger problems.

Soil Vapor Vacuums

Environmental engineers use soil vapor vacuums to extract contaminants from the ground. First, steam is injected into the soil using blowers. Once the steam has absorbed the contaminants, the vacuums are used to suck the contaminated steam, or vapor, from the ground.

Groundwater Pumps

Soil and groundwater often exist in the same spaces. This means that when one is contaminated, the other usually is as well. Environmental engineers use pumps to remove the water from the ground in these instances. A vacuum system in the pump raises the water to the surface. It is then treated before being returned to the earth.

Radiation Detectors

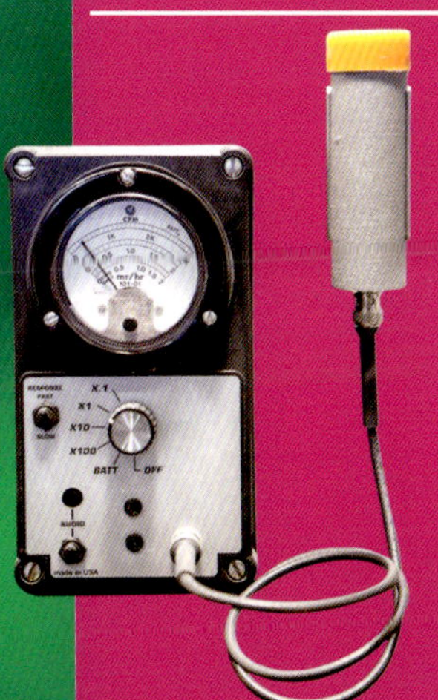

Environmental engineers use radiation detectors in areas where **radioactive** materials may be present. One of the most common places engineers use them is in mines. This is because many minerals contain radioactive elements. If a mine's radiation levels are too high, the engineer can recommend changes. This will help to ensure that the people working there avoid serious health problems.

Biofiltration Systems

Once harmful substances have been found in water, environmental engineers must turn to remediation tools to remove them. Efforts have been made to create tools that do not harm the environment further.

Then

For a long time, water contamination was reversed by adding harsh chemicals. Although this worked, the chemicals could harm the environment or the people using them.

Now

Today, environmental engineers prefer using biofiltration systems. This approach cleans the water through the use of **organisms** that break down and consume contaminants.

The Environmental Engineer's Role

Environmental engineers have been around since civilization itself began. **Archaeologists** have found evidence that the ancient Egyptians built sewage systems to dispose of human waste. Ancient Hindu peoples are known to have added vegetable seeds to their water to make it safe for drinking. The people behind these ideas were among the first environmental engineers.

In 2012, two French engineers embarked on a journey through Europe to prove the viability of the electric car. By the time their trip ended, they had traveled more than 15,000 miles (24,100 kilometers) through 17 countries.

As the world became more complex, the work of environmental engineers also grew more complicated. Today, environmental engineers must find ways to lessen the pollution caused by large-scale manufacturers and factories, and more than 1 billion automobiles.

Technology has made the role of the environmental engineer more difficult in many ways. However, it has also helped engineers find solutions to environmental problems. The development of the electric car, for instance, is one way that technology is proving to help the environment. By easing the strain on the environment, electric cars are also helping environmental engineers.

Electric Cars

Some environmental engineers design electric vehicles (EVs). These vehicles help to reduce pollution. This is because they do not produce harmful exhaust like cars that run on gasoline do.

A **gas-powered** vehicle emits about **5 tons** (4.5 metric tons) of **carbon dioxide** every year.

The **electricity** used to operate an **EV** is about **33%** cheaper than gasoline.

At least **9** electric vehicle models can travel **200 miles** (320 km) on a **single charge**.

Becoming an Environmental Engineer

Environmental engineers share several qualities. They care about the world around them and often step up when a task needs to be done. Just as important is that they have the commitment to see projects through to completion. They want to make the world a better place for themselves and others.

In high school, many environmental engineers were leaders. They may have been captains of sports teams or presidents of clubs. Being a leader does not mean they never failed, however. They learned early on that success often means trying over and over again until they find a solution to a problem. This determination sets environmental engineers up for success once they begin their careers.

Environmental Engineer Salaries

An environmental engineer's salary is based on his or her experience and training. It is also dependent on the job **sector** in which the engineer works.

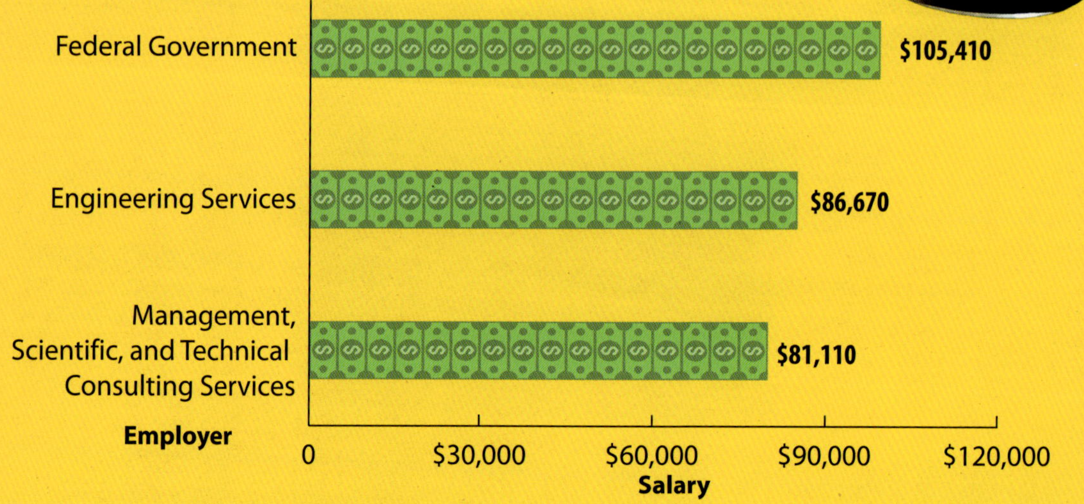

People considering a job in environmental engineering must be comfortable working outdoors and willing to deal with known and unknown hazards.

Is This Career For You?

To prepare for a career in environmental engineering, high school students should seek out classes in advanced math, chemistry, physics, and biology. It is especially important to learn about Earth's many **ecosystems**. Understanding how organisms depend on each other is essential to helping the environment thrive.

Training

Many engineering firms offer **internships** to suitable candidates. These provide people with the opportunity to get real-world experience in environmental engineering. Some universities even offer college credits for taking part in work-study programs.

Education

Most jobs in environmental engineering require a **bachelor's degree**. A person does not have to major in environmental engineering specifically, however. Some people who earn a degree in general engineering or civil engineering may also become environmental engineers.

Application

Companies often prefer to hire environmental engineers who have graduated from colleges that have standing with the Accreditation Board for Engineering and Technology (ABET). Attending one of these schools can widen an environmental engineer's job prospects greatly after graduation.

Career Connections

Plan your environmental engineering career with this activity. Follow the instructions in the steps below to complete the process of becoming an environmental engineer.

A Visit the environmental engineering department of a local university. Talk to the professors. Ask them what they like about their work. Find out where they went to college.

B Decide if this is a job you want to do. Do you want to spend many hours solving environmental problems or challenges?

C Think about the skills you need to be an environmental engineer. People who work in this field must be good at working independently. They should be confident in their abilities and have excellent problem-solving skills.

D Visit an educational fair at a college that teaches engineering classes. Find out what high school classes prepare you to pursue an environmental engineering degree.

1. Think about how you can get work experience while at college. Meet with your professors. Ask them about internships and work-study programs through local companies.

2. Attend career fairs at your college. Talk to people who hire environmental engineers. Ask for advice on how to apply for a job. Find out where their companies post job information.

3. Follow environmental engineering job sites on the internet. Apply for jobs with companies and colleges. Look for internships with state and local governments.

4. Prepare for a job interview. Research the organization. Make a list of questions about the job. Employers will ask questions about your education and work experience.

Quiz

1. What is a carbon footprint?
2. What type of engineer works to reduce health risks in settings such as workplaces?
3. What tool do environmental engineers use to see if a water supply contains dangerous chemicals?
4. What is a brownfield?
5. What is the first step of the scientific method?
6. What does STEM stand for?

7. What did ancient Hindu peoples add to their water to make it safe for drinking?
8. What is an environmental engineer's salary based on?
9. What high school subjects should people take if they want to be environmental engineers?
10. What does the acronym ABET stand for?

Answers

1. The amount of carbon dioxide and other chemicals that a person or business releases into the environment
2. Bio-environmental engineer
3. Water quality monitor
4. An area where chemicals may have contaminated the land
5. Ask a question
6. Science, Technology, Engineering, and Mathematics
7. Vegetable seeds
8. Experience, training, and job sector
9. Math, chemistry, physics, and biology
10. Accreditation Board for Engineering and Technology

Key Words

archaeologists: people who study past peoples through their artifacts

bachelor's degree: the first level of a college program of study

biology: the study of plants and animals

brownfield: an area where chemicals may have contaminated the land

carbon footprint: the amount of carbon dioxide and other chemicals that a person or business releases into the environment

climate change: a long-term change in average weather patterns

contamination: impurities because of pollution

data: facts about something, usually number-related

ecosystems: the animals, plants, and non-living things that make up areas or environments

internships: positions that students take to gain experience, often without pay

laboratories: rooms designed for scientific experiments

natural resources: materials found in nature that people use to make other goods

organisms: any living things

pesticides: chemicals used to protect crops from insects and other pests

radiation: a form of energy that can be very dangerous to health

radioactive: producing energy from the breaking up of atoms

sector: an area of the economy

sewage: wastewater from homes and businesses

wastewater treatment plant: a facility in which contaminants are removed from sewage

Index

Get the best of both worlds.

AV2 bridges the gap between print and digital.

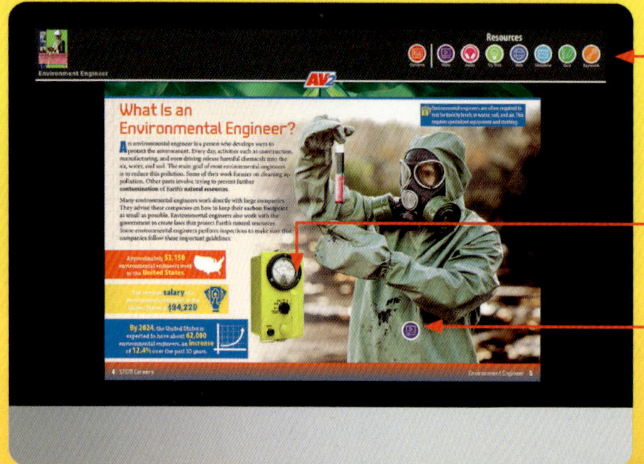

The expandable resources toolbar enables quick access to content including **videos**, **audio**, **activities**, **weblinks**, **slideshows**, **quizzes**, and **key words**.

Animated videos make static images come alive.

Resource icons on each page help readers to further **explore key concepts**.

Published by AV2
14 Penn Plaza 9th Floor
New York, NY 10122
Website: www.av2books.com

Copyright ©2021 AV2
All rights reserved. No part of this publication may be reproduced, stored in a retrieval system, or transmitted in any form or by any means, electronic, mechanical, photocopying, recording, or otherwise, without the prior written permission of the publisher.

Library of Congress Cataloging-in-Publication Data

Names: Gagne, Tammy, author. | Kissock, Heather, author.
Title: Environmental engineer / Tammy Gagne.
Description: New York, NY : AV2, 2021. | Series: Stem careers | Includes index. | Audience: Ages 9-12 | Audience: Grades 4-6
Identifiers: LCCN 2019045339 (print) | LCCN 2019045340 (ebook) | ISBN 9781791116842 (library binding) | ISBN 9781791116859 (paperback) | ISBN 9781791116866 | ISBN 9781791116873
Subjects: LCSH: Environmental engineering--Juvenile literature. | Environmental engineering--Vocational guidance--Juvenile literature.
Classification: LCC TA170 .G34 2021 (print) | LCC TA170 (ebook) | DDC 628.023--dc23
LC record available at https://lccn.loc.gov/2019045339
LC ebook record available at https://lccn.loc.gov/2019045340

Printed in Guangzhou, China
1 2 3 4 5 6 7 8 9 0 24 23 22 21 20

052020
101119

Project Coordinator: Heather Kissock
Designer: Ana María Vidal

Every reasonable effort has been made to trace ownership and to obtain permission to reprint copyright material. The publishers would be pleased to have any errors or omissions brought to their attention so that they may be corrected in subsequent printings.

The publisher acknowledges Getty Images, Alamy, Shutterstock, and iStock as its primary image suppliers for this title.